At the Market

Written by Helen Dineen

Collins

Markets are set up in lots of towns.

3

Markets sell all sorts of things.

You can pick up a loaf.

Or you can get lots of leeks!

How did the leeks get to the market?

We pick leeks at the farm.

The leeks get to the market in a van.

How can you get things at the market?

You will need a card or cash.